Praise For ~~Lead Like Mary~~

"What Deacon Nathan offers in 'Lead Like Mary' is deeply generous. He extends arresting insights, probing questions, and a gentle invitation to enter deeply into the heart of our Mother. Whether you are a seasoned pro, a brand-new disciple, or a reticent leader (raises hand), there is much to explore and pray about in this little tome. Be prepared to be surprised!

Anna Wulfekuhle
Associate Program Leader, Office of Young Adult Outreach - Archdiocese of New York

"'Lead Like Mary' is exactly the kind of motivation leaders need today. In Mary, we learn what it means to be totally disposed to the will of God and having the strength that is capable of overcoming the biggest challenges and disappointments. Deacon Gunn does a wonderful job of providing us with the context surrounding Mary's "Yes" to God's invitation and allows us to reflect further on our daily "yes" to God's plan in our lives, and the mission into which we are called."

Cynthia Psencik
Mentoring Program Director

"As a lifelong Catholic, this book provided insight and reflection that was new, encouraging, and drew me deeper into my faith and devotion. As a woman in leadership, I have been renewed in my calling and have new understanding of how to live it out as an offering to the Lord."

Marisa Avramovich
Young Life US Initiatives Coordinator

"'Lead Like Mary' inspires awareness, validation, and gratitude. It evokes deeper awareness of the ways in which the leadership traits of women, and women of Christian faith - are often different from more masculine approaches. From this awareness flows validation and a deeper sense of value. This book lifts up these approaches and insights as not only legitimate forms of leadership, but values them as essential for a fuller experience of Christian servant leadership. And throughout it all, this work instills deep gratitude to this first disciple, Mary, full of grace, who models for us a path for life-giving leadership, and accompanies us along the journey."

Kathy Goller
Life & Leadership Coach, Teal Horizon Coaching (Founder)

"'Lead like Mary' provides for me a fresh look at the wonder of Mary and her ability to demonstrate leadership coupled with deep love for her family. I have been challenged to rethink my identity and fully embrace my role as a Beloved Child of God. This little book is powerful and could be read over and over for new and enriching nuggets of truth."

Lucy Mills
YoungLives Northeast Divisional Coordinator

To my wife Tammy.

My "ezer kenegdo".

My companion and best friend.

FOREWARD
Carolyn E. Harrison, M.DIV

"I am the Lord's servant. May everything you have said about me come true." Luke 1:38 NLT

The angel Gabriel announced to Mary what was the truest thing about herself. Gabriel extended to Mary God's invitation to collaborate. Mary was "troubled and confused, yet available" and just like that: God's plan of reconciling the world to Himself was set in motion. Mary's fully yielded "yes" points to a life of complete surrender and transformational leadership.

Characteristics of impactful leadership don't always include the quality of a surrendered life. Conversations on leadership tend to center on the contributions of men, and generally include "surrender" on the top ten ways of being a strong leader. In "Lead Like Mary", author Nathan Gunn sets out to elevate feminine leadership by inviting readers to know Mary in a way that reconstructs our understanding of dynamic leadership; particularly leadership energized by a woman's way of knowing. His seven principles of Marian leadership challenge us to reorient our understanding of impactful leadership as lived out by Mary; full of grace, self-aware, and totally surrendered to live into her calling as a leader in God's plan to reconcile the world. Each principle broadens and challenges what we think we know about this first century Palestinian teen girl who has a confidence and self-awareness beyond her years.

This primer for acknowledging under-utilized leadership gifts well serves 21st century men and women. These gifts as laid out by Dc Nathan and lived out by Mother Mary include leading from a secure identity, living fully surrendered to God's love and plans, abiding with a counter-cultural confidence, resting in wonder and contemplation, waiting for direction, following in obedience, and enduring suffering for Love's sake. I've been fortunate to witness Nathan's integration of these Marian leadership principles in his own life. He writes from a place of his own lived experience of surrender to the One who calls him beloved son. I have had the privilege of serving alongside him on mission in NYC and benefit from his commitment to support and equip women in ministry. Dc Nathan's devotion to Jesus is the primary driving force behind his acceptance of the great commission to "go into all the world..." His deep respect for God's mother, which resonates so beautifully through each principle, infuses all of his ministry efforts with tender mercy, grace, and humor. It's no wonder so many people from Syracuse, NY to San Salvador- are drawn to Nathan's expression of the Imago Dei, and long to deepen their own relationship with Jesus. Dc Nathan's Marian-style leadership (full of grace) makes Jesus irresistible.

In the pages that follow, I invite you to experience the beauty of Mary's life and leadership. May you meet her again, and to know her better - the one who models for us the way of leading as fully surrendered daughters and sons of God.

Carolyn Harrison serves as the SoulCare and Initiatives Coordinator for the Young Life Northeast Division.

Bronx Christmas Party – December 2021
Dc Nathan, Carolyn Harrison, Bishop Joseph Espaillat,
Greg Moore (Young Life Chicagoland Regional Director)

Lead Like Mary

A Biblical Primer on Marian Leadership

Deacon Nathan Gunn

The Seven Principles

The First
"Full of grace": Living from our essence

The Second
Mary's "Fiat": Living from surrender

The Third
Mary's Song: Living from counter-cultural confidence

The Fourth
"Pondering them in her heart: Living from wonder and contentment

The Fifth
"Do Whatever He tells you": Living from obedience

The Sixth
"Woman here is your son": Living by being present in suffering

The Seventh
"along with the women and Mary the mother of Jesus": Living by corporate prayer

Post-Script
"Queen of Heaven": the humble vessel becomes the Triumphant

A Different Peter Principle

Perhaps you've heard of the "Peter Principle". It's a simple idea put forward by a management guru named Lawrence Peter that an individual will gain success in one "level" of their career, only to be promoted and then prove to be incompetent at a higher level. While the "Peter Principle" doesn't revolve around the story of Peter – the fisherman from Galilee, it's a fun place to start our conversation.

The apostle Peter is an example of a person who blows through the "Peter Principle". As he is presented in the Gospels, he was lousy at fishing; it turns out he's pretty lousy at most things. But Peter is good at sticking to it and following Jesus. That ability gets him promoted and as it turns out, he did exceedingly well at the next level. Clearly, the "Peter Principle" is not named after our fisherman friend from Galilee. Saint Peter hardly resembles fisherman Peter. The transformation is truly remarkable.

However, when we consider different leadership models in many Western Christian mission fields, one could conclude that all roads lead to the fisherman Peter, and not the saint.

What do I mean?

When one takes a look at the stories, the inspiration, and the messaging from the Gospels that signal to leaders where they might fit in, certain passages and episodes rise to the top. These stories usually center around encounters between Peter from Capernaum and Jesus, the Son of God, from Nazareth.

Which stories am I talking about?

If leaders need to be inspired about calling, we'll watch Peter and his failure to catch fish at night, but highlight his willingness to "put out into the deep to let down his nets."

If we need to hear about having a strong conviction regarding Jesus' identity, we'll hear about Peter's confession of Jesus as Son of God near Caesarea Phillipi.

If we need an example of the dangers of giving into fear, we'll see the shameful denial at the High Priest's courtyard.

If we need an example of bold and yet incomplete faith, we'll see Peter telling Jesus to ask him out on the water – with emphasis on his drowning and distraction from the wind and waves.

Peter's life provides ample examples of meaningful interactions with our Lord. Headstrong. Called. Strong. Weak. Impetuous. Over-confident ("Lord, I'll die with you!"). Peter's three-year odyssey of discipleship is full of ups and downs as well as victories and defeats.

But there's a issue. And it's a massive one.

Peter (well actually "Simon") from Capernaum didn't stay that way. He *changed*.

The problem isn't so much that we tell these stories to inspire leadership. The problem is that we don't tell the other stories. We don't ever seem to finish the story.

When do we ever hear the stories of Saint Peter?

The man from the Book of Acts who prayed in the Upper Room.

The man who preached the Gospel in Jerusalem on the day of the Pentecost and 3,000 came to believe.

The man who walked with John into the Temple at three in the afternoon and healed the beggar with nothing more than the name of Jesus Christ and a handshake.

The man who kept preaching in the Temple and spent nights in jail only to be freed from angels.

And what about the man who sat where Jonah sat on the far east side of the Mediterranean Sea. When Jonah was told to do the unthinkable he hitched a ride on a boat sailing in the opposite direction, but when Peter was given instructions he marched right up to Caesarea Maritime and baptized Cornelius the centurion and his whole household.

What about Saint Peter?

What could we learn about leadership from him? Don't those stories seem to fit better with Christian leadership?

But what's even worse, while we have a myopic focus on the figure of pre-Saint Peter, we have completely ignored a Biblical figure whose leadership far supersedes even the Saint. A person who even the man who sits on Peter's chair in Rome, directly over the grave of Saint Peter from Galilee today *still* defers to.

What have we ever heard about the *leadership* qualities of Mary the Mother of the Son of God?

What mysteries of leadership could we learn if we sat at her feet and told her stories? It's bad enough that we never hear about Peter 2.0: after the cross, the resurrection, the 40 days of visitation, the 10 days of waiting and the Pentecost. But even if we did a deeper dive into the figure of Saint Peter, we still would come up short of the blessing that would be found in considering all that we could learn from Jesus's mother Mary.

To be fair, this idea wasn't something that I had considered for myself until I found myself as the supervisor of numerous women in ministry. I wasn't especially well-equipped to train and support women and their gifted leadership. But I suppose I did "know what I didn't know". My experience taught me that I had a lot to learn and so I watched and listened... a lot.

One of the clear dynamics I learned was that when it came to teaching about leadership from the Gospels, Biblical women were in short supply. The most common story we heard was Mary and Martha. Typically this story was used to emphasize the contemplative over the activist. Most people felt the sting of guilt as they considered their missional calendars and all that was asked of them. Rarely does teaching on this episode the incredible revelation of faith that Martha displays during the episodes surrounding the death of Lazarus.

The other prominent story has been Mary, the perfume adorer who was a former prostitute. This gesture, as extolled by the Lord – led this woman to be honored and revered. Her extreme devotion is rightfully lifted up as worthy of edifying.

But those two women were *it*. If we weren't hearing about Peter's failure to stay afloat, we might hear about Mary over Martha or Mary the "extremely-devoted-former-prostitute".

As someone charged with leading women in ministry, I found these figures difficult to gain access to. We would talk about these stories and themes and it's not that they lacked virtue or meaning – it was simply that in many instances, we were putting a square into a triangle hole. For the people I was leading, bumbling Peter and contemplative Mary didn't have all the answers.

Finally, more out of desperation that inspiration, I considered my own devotion to Mary, the Mother of God and I asked one of the Staff:

"What if we tried to understand and shape your leadership around the figure of Jesus' Mother Mary instead of Peter his apostle?"

She said yes and suddenly, new worlds opened up to us. Perhaps that is a part of her maternal instinct. Mothers create new worlds for us all.

What follows is a Biblical survey of leadership in the school of Mary.

This is introductory work. I am not worthy of unpacking the deep and fathomless treasure of resources found in this remarkable person. In order to help make this work accessible to all people of faith, I will intentionally avoid as much of the controversial dogma surrounding Mary the Mother of God. At the same time, even by simply keeping to the Biblical texts on Mary, we can unpack a treasure trove of goodness.

There are two things I've wondered after years of both working with women and sitting in countless hours of Biblical-based training on leadership.

One: how many women are trying to alter who they are because they don't know that there is a powerful feminine figure that nearly everything runs through?

Two: how many men are leading without any connection to the maternal and feminine aspects of their spirituality that would offer them a tender fullness?

I suppose the last thing I wonder is whether or not we're afraid of her.

She is the Queen of Heaven. Any person who is "clothed with the sun and has the moon under her feet and a crown with twelve stars" at the start of the battle of Armageddon is not to be handled lightly. Maybe she's been too big a figure for people to deal with at all.

The First Principle:

"Full of grace"
Living from our essence

Mary formally enters the narrative in Luke's Gospel. After giving us the story of Elizabeth and Zechariah in stunning detail, Luke tells us:

In the sixth month of Elizabeth's pregnancy, God sent the angel Gabriel to Nazareth, a town in Galilee, to a virgin pledged to be married to a man named Joseph, a descendant of David. The virgin's name was Mary. The angel went to her and said, "Greetings, you who are highly favored! The Lord is with you."

We gain a lot of information from this opening salvo. Mary lived in Nazareth. She was a young woman – a virgin. She was in the process of getting married. First century Jewish engagements were different arrangements than in today's world. Her husband-to-be had a Davidic lineage. We learn right away that an angel named Gabriel was sent by none other than God Himself to visit her.

Luke is a great writer and historian. Doesn't he seem to jam a lot of massive information into one small paragraph? What an introduction!

If anything should make us pause and take notice and then lead us to deep interest in this figure, it's this introduction. While we will return to these aspects over and over, for this first principle, we're going to focus on the angel's words.

"Greetings you who are highly favored. The Lord is with you." That is the 1984 NIV translation. King James translators recorded the message as: "Hail, thou that art highly favored, the Lord is with thee: blessed art thou among women"

At the center of these translations is the original Greek word: *kecharitomene* (κεχαριτωμένη). This word is a page-turner and it's the only place in Scripture that we find it. The root is *"charitoo"* which is the Greek verb to give "grace". Translating all the prefixes and endings is more an art than an exact science. When St Jerome did his first translation of the Greek into Latin in the fourth Century, he came up with *"Ave, gratia plena"*. At least now we know why we all sing "Ave Maria" at Christmas. St Jerome's phrase translates literally to "full of grace". This all makes sense when we take the King James and the St. Jerome together. The formula for the rosary and the "Hail Mary" prayer honors both traditions and translations.

But there's much more.

The tense of the word is the past perfect tense. This means that the action of giving or receiving grace had already occurred– this was not something that was about to happen to her but something that has already been accomplished. And recall– it was fully accomplished.

What Gabriel is identifying is that before he came, before this announcement, even before this Annunciation, Mary was already made "full of grace" in her past. Her *essence* was full of grace.

But then there's even more.

If you look carefully, Gabriel calls Mary this word, not as an adjective but as a TITLE.

Mary is "the *one* who is full of grace". Mary's title is "one whose grace was made full". Mary's entire identity is grace and favor.

Now here is where we want to sit for a minute.

Based on what we just described - and remember, Gabriel said it, not me – Mary is a spectacular person. Again, we're going to avoid the controversial dogma about *how* Mary came to be full of grace in her very being, but we can move forward acknowledging that this is a person for whom every word and action is the fruit of being full of God's grace.

Mary's life in the Gospels and her leadership of the apostles and other followers of Christ was rooted in her identity as full of grace *even before* she was the Mother of God in human history. Her ministry to the world flowed out of her identity as full of grace and favor.

And this is both the invitation and the challenge for us.

What if our ministry to the world flows from our essential identity? What if– before any formation or training or classes or seminars– what if that core essence is the place that we draw from for our own ministry?

The horror of this reality is the damaged identities that so many of us live with. So many people, especially those who have come to Christ and are beginning to take their first steps into Christian leadership still experience the damage done to their core identities, whether as children or young adults. So much dysfunction exists in our homes and communities that very few people get through that toxic gauntlet with their core identity intact.

As we begin to unpack the idea that we minister out of our essences, we need to step back and pause at the power of that conviction.

A word about "essence" is important here. The Greeks had an idea called the "esse". We might call it our "being". It's our natural state, who we are if we're not doing anything. Detach all the roles and all the responsibilities and all the actions – when you're "being" and not "doing" – that's your *esse*.

This isn't your emotions. For many of us, when we actually slow down from all the commotion, our emotions finally flood to the surface. We might even avoid that pause for fear of what may come up! Consider how much time we spend in the modern age distracting ourselves with useless inputs. But it's important to understand that this emotional settling is not our essence – it's not our state of being – it's our emotional life and health working itself out.

Another word for essence is ontology: the state of our being. We always say, "How you doing?" or, "How you been?" I don't think I've ever been asked, "How do you describe your ontological nature?"

BUT WE SHOULD ASK!

Below the relationships and the activities and the emotions and even the thoughts, deep down in the bowels of our very human existence is our essence, our ontology, our state of being.

For Mary, her state of being, way down there, was "full of grace". What a gift! And everything that we will see in her life and ministry is going to flow from that foundational reality.

But what does that mean for us and our leadership?

If we were going to follow Mary and her leadership, we are going to have to discover the truth of our own essence, our own ontology – our own state of being.

What would Gabriel say to you if God sent him to your cave today?

What words do you imagine he would say?

Jesus had this happen to him as well. He had just come out of the water at the Jordan River, baptized by his cousin John (Elizabeth's kid). Out of nowhere, there was a voice:

"You are my Son, whom I love; with you I am well pleased."

Thankfully the Greek here is pretty basic and it speaks to the mystical simplicity of Jesus identity as the incarnate Son of God.

Beloved Son.

The significance of this declaration of Jesus's essence at this moment is that Jesus has yet to do any of his ministry. So far, he's just been a young man living with his family in Nazareth. We haven't seen him since he was twelve years old staying behind in the Temple. By human standards, he's more than a late bloomer– he's late to the game. Unless you're dialed into the fact that David didn't become King of Israel until he hit age thirty and perhaps Jesus was following his ancestor's mold. But here at the river, on the eve of his public ministry, God intervenes to remind him of his beloved state of being. What a beautiful and moving scene!

Mary's ministry flowed from her essence as full of grace.

Jesus' ministry flowed from his essence as the beloved Son of God.

If we remember this identity, we'll hear Jesus talk this way about himself and His Father over and over and over again.

He lived out of his identity.

Now that's beautiful for Jesus and Mary – but what about us?

This first principle has two elements to accept. First, that we have an essence to our existence that accepts what God says and does in us and for us regardless of what we've said or done. Second, that our ministry leadership flows from that essence. Moving forward, might I suggest a few steps?

Can you identify your current ontological state? If someone asked you, what is your essential identity? Where does it come from? How would you respond?

This is a deep and necessary wrestling.

Of course, Mary's surrogate son John tells us pretty plainly how we should see ourselves:

"Behold the manner of love that Father has lavished on us that we should be called the children of God! And that is what we are!"

It would appear that John's extensive time with both Jesus as an apostle and Mary as a son had taught him the conviction that we should view ourselves as sons and daughters of God. This core-essential-identity does not come from us– it is given to us by God Himself.

Are you comfortable with accepting God's designation as His Beloved Child as your essential existence?

Even the word "essential" points to our own linguistic connection to our "esse" being, well – essential!

Of course, there are reasonable hang-ups based on whatever your own story with family or parents or father may be, but is it possible for you to imagine that the beginning center of your life – the source of everything else that flows, comes from your acceptance as Beloved Child of God?

As you explore this possibility, you'll find more and more attributes to your essential nature. Qualities like forgiven, restored, empowered, accompanied. If you explore this relationship between God's creating Voice and your existence, you'll maybe hear that you are eternal, beloved and cherished. You may find that that God is the source of all change and that He is in fact changing you and your essence to become more in line with His vision of who you are and what makes you exist.

For Mary, she was forever full of grace.
For Jesus, he was forever God's Beloved Son.
For us, we are the Beloved Children of God and that essential identity changes everything.

Your own identity as Child of God was inherent in your creation but solidified in your baptism. Emerging from the waters of baptism, you received every grace offered to any divine child in the family of Jesus. Your ontological reality was sealed by Christ on the cross.

As we grow more comfortable with accepting our true essence as God's children, our leadership can begin to flow in a healthy way from that core.

Mary's life wasn't just "full of grace" as some sort of transcendent place of being that she pulled into or elevated herself to. She was "full of grace" incarnate. She was the beauty of that mysterious word – but with skin on.

The same was true with Jesus. Jesus was the Beloved Son of God in a mystical sense within the Trinity but it was the earthiness and humility of the Incarnation of that essence that changed everything.

The challenge is for us to follow the footsteps of Mary and Jesus and begin to live out of our essential identity.

It's key here to pause and consider the difference between essence and personality. There are some wonderful personality studies and tools that exist like Strengths Finders, Myers-Briggs and the Enneagram. Each of these proven tools serve a wonderful utility for the purpose of identifying natural strengths and tendencies. They are particularly helpful and effective when used in team settings so that everyone can appreciate the differences and uniqueness of each individual. With good communication in place, these personality tools can go a long way to helping teams function with much greater authenticity and effectiveness.

However, what is being offered here is something even deeper. Believe it or not, personalities and strengths can change. They can harden or grow narrower, but they can also grow softer and broader. To a certain degree, how a person functions in relationship to their own essential identity can affect their personality given any particular situation. Oftentimes, who we present to the world changes as we adapt to the roles we serve in. While it is a good and positive step to understand your personality tendencies, imagine the depth of impact if you understood your core essence!

As we move forward, we'll find that Mary's words and actions were in deep connection to the deepest reality of her soul. I have a sense of her personality, but it's really my own sense. You may read these stories and come up with a different idea. Regardless of our read on her personality, we will still find her "full of grace".

If the people you lead were to fill out a personality survey, they would probably get pretty close to identifying how you operate. But what if they filled out a survey that asked them to consider your own sense of your essential identity? What would they observe? Below your personality is your existence. How you feel and what you think rest in large part on the reality of what you choose to believe about your essential existence. How does that conviction come through?

People experienced Mary as full of grace.
People experienced Jesus as beloved son of the Father.
How do people experience you?

The Second Principle:
"Mary's Fiat"
Living from surrender

As we follow the narrative of the Annunciation in Luke's Gospel, we learn that the angel's greeting startled Mary. Luke tells us that Mary was "greatly troubled" and wondered what this all might mean. Given Mary's humanity, that response seems completely reasonable. How could she possible expect what Gabriel would say next?

But the angel said to her, "Do not be afraid, Mary; you have found favor with God. You will conceive and give birth to a son, and you are to call him Jesus. He will be great and will be called the Son of the Most High. The Lord God will give him the throne of his father David, and he will reign over Jacob's descendants forever; his kingdom will never end."

We may be familiar with the details of this message and of course we know the outcome. But to sit in Mary's seat for a moment allows for even a small portion of the immense weight of this message to sink in. What exactly was being proposed?

Mary was a righteous woman. She was young. She was virtuous. She was living as a poor person in a small village. Nazareth was to function as its name sake; "new shoot". As Jews came back from exile from

Babylon and especially as the Greeks and Romans conquered their country, Nazareth was to be a new settlement, a new growth, a new outcropping.

Remember in that epic passage from Isaiah when he tells us: "There shall come forth a shoot from the stump of Jesse"? The Hebrew word for "new shoot" is nēṣer. What is fascinating is that "neser" is the same root for the town of Mary, Joseph, and Jesus: Nazareth, was literally, a new shoot town. Sitting high on the cliffs above the Valley of Meggido, Mary must have spent hours walking through the rocky and uneven fields. Life would have been hard in this small mountain village. There was the Mediterranean to the west and the Sea of Galilee to the east. Across this geography, people would come and go with regularity as Nazareth was in proximity to the major trade routes.

Against this rough and spartan backdrop, Mary and her family had managed to find her a nice suitor. We don't know much about her fiancé's background at this point, but we know that he was a laborer and he proved to be an exceedingly honorable man.

At this point in their relationship, she is betrothed to marry Joseph but our contemporary sense of engagement falls a little short. In accepting the engagement, Mary and her family entered into a one-year preparation period that ended with the ceremony and the consummation of their marriage. At the moment of the angel's interruption, culturally, Mary is Joseph's.

And though Mary is young, she is not simple. Look at all the loaded information that Gabriel drops on her lap:

"You will conceive and give birth to a son."

"You will call him Jesus"

"He will be called the Son of the Most High"

"God will put him on David's throne"

"His kingdom will have no end"

All of this speech is Messiah-language and for sure, Mary would have been familiar with the concepts of the Jewish Messiah for her day. Without speculating improperly, we can safely assume that Mary and her family were well aware of the constant groaning and yearning of the people of God, especially in the north, for God's Messiah to come and restore all things.

But these claims of Gabriel seem outrageous. Mary's response doesn't seem to initially elaborate or consider any personal consequences or fears. If we could simplify the angel's message it would be:

You will conceive a son. Name him Jesus. He will be the Messiah.

Something incredible emerges immediately. Let's slow the story down.

Mary seems to innately grasp that this Jesus-Messiah-Son is not going to come through relations with Joseph. This would have been the most natural thing to assume.

Naturally, we would completely understand if Mary's response was along the lines of:

"Thank you for the great news! The wedding is in six months. Thanks for the heads up! I'll let Joseph know the good news." This would have been so reasonable especially since Joseph is from David – the Messiah's bloodline.

But, as we learn, Mary has a keen sense that this action is present tense and that she is being asked to participate as Mary – the one who is betrothed, but not fully married. Listen to her question...

"How will this be," Mary asked the angel, "since I am a virgin?"

There are so many remarkable considerations from this clear and direct question.

First – Mary asks the obvious sex-ed question. She does not shy away from the physical and biological reality of the proposition. Though Mary is "full of grace" – she is not prudish or ignorant and unaware. She is direct and she is honest and she is truthful. Given the most incredible proposition ever given to any person in human history, her follow-up question is simple and clear.

Second, Mary's question reveals her understanding of the gravity of the present moment. As was mentioned, the thought of a child in the future wasn't outrageous for someone who was betrothed for marriage. However, Mary reveals that she intrinsically understood that Gabriel meant NOW. There was something within her or in Gabriel's message that convinced Mary that Gabriel was talking about something that was about to happen.

The reason that realization is so significant is because there is a mammoth difference between Gabriel's proposition to a married woman and an engaged woman. Had Mary presumed that she would get pregnant from Joseph and their son would be the Jewish Messiah, they are in for the ride of their lives but her own life wouldn't be at stake. In fact, given the angel's greeting, that understanding of Gabriel's message makes a ton of sense. If Jesus is to be the natural son of Mary and Joseph and he will be the Messiah of Israel – then she truly is highly favored; it would all make sense.

But, as she infers, if this pregnancy is to come about through other means, then Mary's participation in the divine Messiah business might cost her everything. By agreeing to host the Messiah in her womb and birth him into the world, Mary puts her entire life in the hands of Joseph and thousands of years of customs that would be stacked against her.

Given Mary's understanding and the stakes at hand for her personally, her question is even more courageous and bold. In response, Gabriel replies:

"The Holy Spirit will come on you, and the power of the Most High will overshadow you. So the holy one to be born will be called the Son of God. Even Elizabeth your relative is going to have a child in her old age, and she who was said to be unable to conceive is in her sixth month. For no word from God will ever fail."

Now, I'm not one to pick on an angel. And I am a man so I have no right to claim any understanding of these matters. So I offer this reaction with all humility.

Doesn't Gabriel's answer here seem a little vague?

The Holy Spirit and the "power of the Most High"?

I get the "holy one will be called the Son of God"– that makes sense. Joseph will clearly not be the father. This child will come into the world through divine means. And I even understand the offering of Elizabeth for verification; God has a history of assisting women who were barren or in need. This isn't the first time that we've heard the idea of a woman becoming pregnant outside the bounds of normalcy. What is new is the idea that Mary will become pregnant by God.

I simply want to offer, that from where I sit, it seems that Gabriel was vague on details. I can imagine a myriad of questions that his response creates. In my mind, there are at least two remaining issues that Gabriel's answer doesn't address for Mary.

-What exactly does "overshadowing" mean?

-What does she do about Joseph and the Law?

Mary has already proven herself to be sharp. Her first words in Scripture are clear – "How is this going to happen?" Hidden in her first question is an indictment of her relative Zechariah's response to his angel at the Temple. Luke's storytelling genius is on full display here. He works through juxtaposition chapter after chapter. Let's return to chapter 1 of the Gospel.

Zechariah was a priest. He was in liturgy. He was in the Temple. He had been praying for a child for years. His angel gave him the legitimately good news that his prayers were answered. The role is right. The moment is right. The setting is right. The news is good.

But Zechariah, with all that goodness and "rightness" going for him, fumbles the moment. He asked Gabriel, "How can I be *sure* of this?" And then he points out that he and his wife are too old.

Consider Mary.

She's not a priest. She's not at the Temple. She's not leading liturgy. We don't know if she's been praying for years for a child. And yet, her response is acceptable to Gabriel; it was a question that was "full of grace".

There is a huge gap between "How can this be?" and "How can I be sure?"

Given Mary's innate understanding of the present proposal, she knew what the cost was. She knew that her participation put everything in jeopardy. For a young woman in Nazareth in the first century, her engagement to Joseph was everything. Her connection to him meant security and safety. The entire society had organized women's existence around men. Mary had only two boxes to get checked in her life: one – get married, two – have children. But the order really mattered.

Gabriel is silent about Joseph. Given the weight of the proposition and the apparent understanding that Mary has displayed, I'm struck that Gabriel doesn't give her at least some comfort or instructions about how she will survive her pregnancy. But somehow– almost

19

mystically– Mary doesn't need such reassurances. She rises above her uncle's disposition ("How can I be sure?"). It's not that Mary isn't aware, but she simply doesn't seem to need to know the plan. Perhaps she had the liberty with Gabriel to ask more questions. Perhaps he would have been forthcoming. But Mary is Mary– there's none like her. She simply responds in complete and total reckless *surrender*:

"I am the Lord's servant," Mary answered. "May your word to me be fulfilled." Then the angel left her.

Every time I consider what was at stake for this brave young woman and how little information Mary was afforded, I am filled with awe and wonder at how she ascended to give such a total and complete response.

Do you remember the first principle? Mary's essence was grace. Remember how we explored what it would mean to operate out of our essence as beloved children of God?

This is the first lesson. Let Mary teach you.

As the "most favored one" of God most high – you don't need to ask a lot of clarifying questions. You simply live out of your identity – "I am the Lord's servant."

Mary knew who she was. Her submission is actually an affirmation. Her affirmation was a beautiful and triumphant pronouncement of what God had already done in her life and her self-actualization. She wasn't simply willing; she was fully engaged and actively surrendered to God's word and will in her life. Though I can speculate about how a continued conversation with Gabriel might have proceeded, Mary didn't need it. She heard everything she needed to because she was living in her essence.

So once again, we receive an invitation and a challenge.

What if we were willing to live in our essential identity as children of God? If we found ourselves accepting that invitation, then we are challenged to live a life of surrender to the reality of who we are and who God is.

Living a life that leads like Mary means that we are deeply content and deeply surrendered to the freedom that comes from knowing who we are in Christ.

Seen in the light of this Gospel – total surrender is an invitation to total freedom. Mary's only agenda is God's agenda. Mary's hopes for her life are intimately woven into God's hopes for her. Mary's very life is in the Hand of God and she appears ready to rejoice. By living out of her ontological reality, her state of being, she is able to joyfully surrender her very life as a grace received from God.

Obviously, for us to move forward in this manner will take some real work, some real wrestling at the core of who we are. We might ask ourselves where we are tempted to take control of our lives. Are we concerned with our reputation? Our futures? Our images? The identity we project to the world? Do we find ourselves living behind the curtain like Zechariah – explaining to God why the miraculous and beautiful things that He wants to do might not work? Or do we find ourselves open and free before God to say "yes" to whatever His Word is because HE is the one who said it.

But let's remember– Jesus makes this offer to all of his followers. This privilege is not exclusive to Mary. Recall the episode from Matthew's Gospel when Jesus is spending time with Mary and a crowd shows up. Jesus says (pointing to the disciples), "Here are my mother and my brothers. For whoever does the will of my Father in heaven is my brother and sister and mother." Wow– what an incredible invitation!

I'm not suggesting that gaining a life that is this fully and deeply surrendered to God is easy. But I can suggest that it does become easier. The first steps of the journey are the hardest. The very awareness of this type of freedom and direction may be the most startling part. Let me put it another way.

For many of us at some point, we "came to Christ" or "gave our lives to Jesus Christ." So many beautiful disciples of Jesus can articulate a moment or a process by which they came to know Jesus personally. And after this initial joyful surrender, many of us became aware that Jesus wanted more. Our decision or commitment to Him was meant to be in everything *and* all the time. The challenge to "pick up our cross and follow Him" in our own "costly discipleship" is real and it can be intense. Along the way, we may look to peers or other heroes of the faith to aid us in our struggle to surrender more of our lives to Christ.

My own experience of self-surrender has accelerated and my own understanding of the freedom of surrender has been more impactful, because of my relationship to Mary and her "fiat". This story has caused me to reorient my discipleship to the reality of who I actually am *in Christ*. In the end, my discipleship is less and less about me – and more and more about Him. As I lean more into the words that He speaks about me, I am invited to heed St Paul's words to the Romans to "not conform to the patterns of this world but be transformed by the renewing of our mind". See how Paul is emphasizing our mindset? Mary's model and companionship on my own journey of self-surrender have been both an inspiration and a consolation.

Seen in this light, my leadership has completely changed. Leading like Mary in self-surrender meant that I began to see people and struggles and suffering as a means to surrender. Where certain situations might have caused me to tighten up and grip harder, her invitation was to loosen up and let go. In fact, the very impulse to grab and hold taut became a trigger for me to relax, remember my true identity, and to let go.

People are not under your leadership for you to control. They are eternal creatures, loved and beloved by God – a gift to you as someone to nurture, shape and direct with God's loving Spirit. Surrendering your own will to God's Word for those you lead is a beautiful and freeing invitation. What a different paradigm to consider!

Leading like Mary in self-surrender has many dimensions. We find ourselves in a deep dive about our own willingness to say "yes" and surrender to the Word of God in our life. But as we journey deeper, we are invited to loosen our own grip on those we lead and impact. We can offer them to Christ and begin to identify more strongly with God's Word about them too.

I can recall the early days when my friend and I began to see ourselves and people this way. What a gift it was to leave our old views behind, to loosen the idol of control and yield more and more to the Holy Spirit.

What could happen in your life if you began to lead like Mary?

The Third Principle:
"Mary's Song"
Living from a counter-cultural confidence

Powerful women have been ignoring the edicts of governments since time began. Let's not forget that when Pharaoh became concerned that the Israelites were becoming too numerous, he instructed all the sons to be killed by the midwives.

The first acts of defiance came from Shiphrah and Puah. They saved the Hebrew boys and shrugged before Pharaoh with the story: "What can we do? Hebrew women give birth before we can get there." Shrewd storytelling to a man who may not have known the details around such things as labor and delivery.

Then we get another mother.

She was from the tribe of Levi – the tribal birth line of priests. She gave birth and was able to protect him for three months. Knowing that his days were numbered, she brought him down "to the river" and released him in a basket. But this wasn't just any old send-off.

Moses' mother released him into the Nile just upriver from Pharaoh's palace at an hour when Pharaoh's own daughter came down to cool herself in the waters. Moses' mother preserved her son's life and set the direction for his safety and future. And she did all this against the backdrop of rebellion to one of the world's all-time empires.

As we'll soon find out, Mary has a bit of that heritage in her story, as well.

Luke's narrative around Mary takes a decisive turn. After learning that she would become miraculously pregnant with the Jewish Messiah, Luke tells us that Mary got ready and hurried to a town in Judea and entered the house of Zechariah and greeted Elizabeth. While we can't state definitively where Elizabeth lived, we can be certain that it was a multi-day journey across treacherous lands. Our modern ears love a scandal and I know that I am hungry for the details of Mary's conversation with Joseph, but Luke doesn't have that critical moment for us. Instead, she makes haste and heads south for the safety of her kin.

We can only imagine— we can only place ourselves in her shoes— a poor young woman in Palestine, attached to a caravan of travelers, alone in the world and in the ever-present danger of strange lands and people. Mary is a woman who carries not only the Savior of her people but also the weight of the world. Can we possibly fathom her shared delight and terror? In a moment that should be fraught with anxiety and anticipation, there are no answers to her reasonable longings.

As she enters into Elizabeth's house, the greeting of her relative must have brought her tender reassurance:

When Elizabeth heard Mary's greeting, the baby leaped in her womb, and Elizabeth was filled with the Holy Spirit. In a loud voice she exclaimed: "Blessed are you among women, and blessed is the child you will bear! But why am I so favored, that the mother of my Lord should come to me? As soon as the sound of your greeting reached my ears, the baby in my womb leaped for joy. Blessed is she who has believed that the Lord would fulfill his promises to her!"

Here, I'd love to pause and do a deep dive into the phrase, "filled with the Holy Spirit". The Greek word is definitive. We see it three times. It is the same phrase as with the Apostles at Pentecost, Peter preaching in the Temple and the apostle Paul in Paphos. For those who live in the Pentecostal or charismatic side of the family of God – this designation is a thrill. This woman was not only full of child – the prophet of the Son of the Most High, but also with the third Person of the Trinity.

This is a potent conversation between two very powerful women.

Within this framework – we get the first foretaste of the intoxicating ingredient of counter-cultural confidence:

JOY - "The baby in my womb leaped for joy".

Blessings are being showered on Mary from a woman who is full of the Holy Spirit and carries the voice of one who will be preaching in the wilderness. For all the concerns and unknowns that Mary must have experienced, can we fathom the comfort and solace that came from being in the presence of another woman who was full of the Holy Spirit and greeted her with joy?

This speaks immediately to our leadership in today's world.

How do we greet people?

Do we welcome with joyful and pregnant anticipation of good things to come?

Or are we people who bring deep concerns and gloomy forecasts, weighing people down with all the unknowns of our calling and hopes?

There is a medicinal effect available for us as we consider these powerful women, laughing together in joyful anticipation of God's goodness. Many of us spend countless hours in conversations over coffees or salads, on sidelines and in parking lots. What is the flavor of those encounters?

For us to grasp the full power of Mary's encounter with Elizabeth, we have to listen to her song and the deep and rich context from which she sang:

"My soul glorifies the Lord
and my spirit rejoices in God my Savior,
for he has been mindful
of the humble state of his servant.
From now on all generations will call me blessed,
for the Mighty One has done great things for
me—
holy is his name.
His mercy extends to those who fear him,
from generation to generation.
He has performed mighty deeds with his arm;
he has scattered those who are proud in their
inmost thoughts.
He has brought down rulers from their thrones
but has lifted up the humble.
He has filled the hungry with good things
but has sent the rich away empty.
He has helped his servant Israel,
remembering to be merciful
to Abraham and his descendants forever,
just as he promised our ancestors."

The Catholic Church is so struck by this song that the litany is repeated every night in the Evening Prayer of the Liturgy of the Hours. These lyrics have struck a chord with hopeful believers around the world for thousands of years. But, in truth, Mary's words are deeply rooted in the song of another powerful woman from Israel's history.

Before there was a righteous King in Israel before Samuel went and found David, there was a woman named Hannah who could not get pregnant. She spent hours in prayer, lamenting with God and wrestling with Yahweh, pleading for God to intercede and spare her from the shame of barrenness.

God only knows how many women around the world have joined in the prayers of Hannah.

The parallels between Hannah and Mary are abundant.

While Hannah's barren womb is a source of social and public shame, Mary's womb's fullness will be the root of her social humiliation. In both instances, the priests (Eli and Zechariah) are on the edges of the action while the women are more open and responsive to the miraculous words and deeds of God. In both instances, the child born was a son. Likewise, both Hannah and Mary dedicate their sons in the Temple to God. While Hannah petitions God for a child, she surrenders him to the service of the Lord in the Temple after receiving him. In contrast, Mary's surrender was to receive her son and when Jesus is left in the Temple, she returns to find him and take him with her.

Finally, both women sing a song to God and begin those songs with words of praise. Where Hannah sings, "My heart rejoices in the Lord; in the Lord my horn is lifted high... for I delight in your deliverance", Mary responds with, "My soul glorifies the Lord and my spirit rejoices in God my Savior".

Isn't it significant that at the beginning of the movements of King David and Jesus the Christ, the priests and men are silent? Zechariah is muted by the angel and Jesus' father Joseph doesn't utter a single word in all the Gospel accounts. Instead, like Mary Magdalene, the "Apostle of the Apostles" running from the tomb to Peter and John on Easter Sunday, Mary and Hannah are the protagonists *and* the mouthpieces of God's incarnate actions in the affairs of people. When God wanted to save the world, he started with the employ of holy women who were open to proclaim and sing the movements of His Spirit.

We cannot miss this point. This isn't about equity, it's about prophecy.

Hannah saw restorative change for the least on the horizon as a result of her child. So did Mary. When Hannah sings, "Those who were full hire themselves out for food, but those who were hungry hunger no more"

Mary mirrors, "He has filled up the hungry with good things but he has sent the rich away empty." Likewise, Hannah identifies that "He raises the poor from the dust and lifts up the needy from the ash heap; he seats them with princes and has them inherit a throne of honor" while Mary declares, "He has brought down rulers from their thrones and lifted up the humble". Clearly, both women's praise is not simply thanksgiving for the miraculous conception of their children, but perhaps more significantly, interpretive verse regarding the restorative correction of the world order that will occur as a result of their pregnancies.

When we consider these heroic women together we immediately see their shared humility. Mary emphasizes her existence as a "humble servant". Hannah echoes that same lowly position. These hopeful and counter-cultural confidences don't come to these women by virtue of their education or training or degrees or bank accounts or even social media. These women don't find their strength to declare God's redemptive Kingdom on the basis of their accolades or the endorsements of others. They don't find their strength in their "followers" or even their friends.

The strength and source of their rebellion against the ways of the world is found in their convictions about who they are before God and what He has said He will do through them.

Slow down and read that last sentence again.

Without Hannah's prayers of lament and justice, there is no future line of David: there is no "Eleazar father of Matten, father of Jacob, father of Joseph…" Without Mary's "yes" as a humble servant of the God Most High – there is no Jewish Messiah and fulfillment of the Kingdom of God on earth.

But these women aren't done. As we listen to their joyous songs, we hear deeper tones– the prelude of the rebellion of God's Kingdom.

Hannah's song talks about the wild reversal of the fortunes of two distinct groups: "The bows of the warriors are broken, but those who stumbled are armed with strength." While the downtrodden are lifted up, Hannah validates them with further encouragement: "It is not by strength that one prevails; those who oppose the Lord will be shattered." Consider how powerfully this song must reverberate with those who have suffered oppression across thousands of years and across all the earth. Oppressed people can easily identify their own enemies and yearn for the reality that God is singing about. Her faith in God as liberator is resolute.

In the same manner, Mary tells the audience that God "has performed mighty deeds with his arm… He has brought down rulers from their thrones". While Mary's imagery does not identify direct military imagery, the geopolitical reality of Mary's song presents as drastic a reversal as Hannah's.

Stemming from their identities as God's humble servants, they see God doing miraculous work in their lives and they tie that work into the counter-cultural, world-altering, Kingdom-incarnate movement on earth. Out of their humility and God's Hand, they see the world forever changed for the better. I'm reminded of the Psalmist's beautiful imagery:

Love and faithfulness meet together;
    righteousness and peace kiss each other.
Faithfulness springs forth from the earth,
    and righteousness looks down from heaven.
The LORD will indeed give what is good,
    and our land will yield its harvest.
Righteousness goes before him
    and prepares the way for his steps.

There is such a joyful hope in these women's songs. These are the not songs of the entitled or the "privileged". These are the not the lyrics of women who are demanding what is rightfully theirs. These are not the words of gritty women who see the world through the lens of some sort of dialectic of "haves" and "have-nots".

These women of God are rejoicing in God as their Provider and King while He is making them *mothers*.

Against the modern backdrop of a blaring cacophony that oftentimes misrepresents true femininity, biology, reality of genetics and thousands of years of lived reality, Mary and Hannah sing their songs as women warriors who saw a hopeful vision of the future of the world because of the Hand of God on the sons they carried in their wombs. They did not succumb to some sort-of demented misreading of their times or their realities but embraced who God was, who they were and who their boys would be. To call this moment somehow "political" would be pure foolishness.

The world would be saved by the humble actions of mothers.

Salvation would come into the world through a birth canal.

Mary's confidence came from knowing that regardless of what was going to happen up in Nazareth, God was on her side. When I hear Mary's song, I hear:

"If Yahweh has my back, bring it on."

We have seen how she was full of grace. We have seen how she was fully surrendered. Now we hear Mary full of confidence.

But don't get sidetracked: her confidence isn't in her own skills or personality or training, her confidence is completely rooted in what God said He would do. Her confidence is rooted in Hannah's song and Hannah's story and David's Kingdom. Mary knows her history. She knows her roots. She knows which family is going to give birth to the Jewish Messiah. She knows who Joseph's father is. Mary is no fool – blindly praising God with no rational cause.

But she is completely counter-cultural.

Let's finish where we started.

We just witnessed an embrace between a woman who was "full of the Holy Spirit" and pregnant with the chosen prophet of Jewish Messiah and a woman who an angel identified by the TITLE "full of grace" who carrying the child of the Son of the Most High God.

Is this not the most powerful meeting between two women in human history?

And notice – the only "men" present are in the wombs. Zechariah and Joseph are silent on the matter.

But for all of that spiritual firepower, Mary is still a young, uneducated, poor girl from a nothing frontier village whose life is in legitimate danger due to the scandal of her pregnancy. She is a nobody from nowhere with nothing.

AND YET– she sings with joy that God is going to turn the world upside down and bring restorative justice to the poor and throw rulers off their thrones!

Where else can she possibly get the audacious confidence to sing that song *EXCEPT* for her complete and total faith and identity in the One who chose her? Which brings us to ourselves.

What about us?

What are we putting our confidence in? Do we even have any reason for confidence? Are you hoping that this degree, this position, this next opportunity will finally fulfill the change you are looking for? Or put that in reverse, what are you blaming for holding you back?

Are you using others in your leadership to manipulate your own lack of confidence in what God Himself will do?

What is the longing and lament of your heart? Can you find the courage to be real and honest enough before God in His Temple to humble yourself to His Word for you in your life?

Do you want to waste another minute, hour, or day chasing a "word" that is not His? Who else have you allowed to enter into your head that is not Him?

Do you have a brother or sister that sings Mary and Hannah's song with you? For you? Who else is listening to this music in your life that you can bond with, and celebrate and rejoice in all that God has done and is doing?

Do you feel entitled to things because the world says so OR do you live in confidence in the reality of the way things ARE because God has said so.

Finally – in what ways do these women and their songs inspire you to surrender your life to God's counter-cultural Kingdom because of what He has said and what He has done? How can these powerful women's songs affect the world we imagine for those we lead? What song is on our lips?

These meditations are piercing but they are real.

As we will see, Mary is tender and Mary is kind, but she does not joke around – especially when we are talking about Her Son and His Kingdom.

The Fourth Principle:
"Pondered them in her heart"
Living from wonder and contentment

Where Luke and the other Gospel writers are vague on details regarding what happened with Mary and Joseph after she returned to Nazareth, the historian-doctor gives us now-famous information and timestamps for the circumstances around Jesus' birth.

We learn that Joseph was required to travel south to Bethlehem to the village and land of his people. This journey was not easy nor timely. We learn about all the geopolitical players and the local and imperial powers at play. We are forced to ask ourselves why Joseph felt compelled to bring his nine-month pregnant wife on such a dangerous journey. Could it be that Joseph somehow felt that Mary was safer in his company on the perilous pilgrimage than at home in the company of his and her family?

Bethlehem was a small shepherd village on the hills outside of Jerusalem. The sheep that traveled up and down these pastures would be taken out by shepherds for days and weeks at a time, sometimes traveling as far away as the region around En Gedi where David hid from murderous Saul. While King Herod built his great fortress up high at Masada, the Bedoin shepherds learned the crevices and caves and deep mossed-lined waterfalls. The shepherds knew where the springs were and how to live in a barren landscape. This was the setting where Samuel had picked out a handsome young boy named David and anointed him as the future shepherd King of Israel.

Bethlehem is a village that is pregnant in the history of Israel. The town's name means "House of Bread". Consider how much goodness the world has reaped from this single little village. God's voice showed up in an unexpected way at one of the most significant moments in their history. And yet, as the people of Israel were straining and looking and crying for Messiah, they weren't looking at places like Nazareth and Bethlehem– all eyes were wrongly focused on the Temple and Jerusalem.

When Mary and Joseph arrived in Bethlehem, a village full of kin and blood relatives, no one was able to offer a room or a bed to this young couple. Hospitality is among the most significant virtues and values of the Jewish people, both now and then. Opening one's home to the traveler or friend in need is a universal virtue across the Middle East to this day. We don't know the details, but the fact that Joseph and Mary were pressed into a stable because there was no room for them is an unusual stain on the people gathered in Bethlehem. We have to wonder what could have been on the hearts and minds of those who pushed this young couple to the edges of the community in their moment of need.

Remember, these are relatives, Joseph's bloodlines. Mary and Joseph are shut out by those who should have at least felt obligated to bring them in.

But this is the stirring of God's Hand in Bethlehem. The rejection of the people at Bethlehem fits all the better; it teaches us and startles us. How often have we pushed the Incarnation of God to the margins? How often have I decided that Jesus or the Spirit must come in a certain way or in a certain people and certainly *NOT* in *that* place or with *those* people?

As a husband and father and as one who was present in the room for the births of both my sons, I cannot imagine the intensity and pressure of this moment. No two labors or deliveries are the same and I cannot speak to Joseph or Mary's understanding of what would take place. However, I can say with confidence as someone who has been bedside, the intensity of emotions for Joseph must have been significant. Luke allows us to fill in our own blanks, but the pressure and strain must have been incredible. I know that I felt emotions that I had never experienced, and we were fully supported and celebrated. It's not fair to impose our modern expectations and experiences on this couple, but as we move towards Mary's ability to "treasure these things and ponder them in her heart", we can at least place ourselves in their position and see an experience that was full of disappointment, surprise, exhaustion and jubilation. Fill in the blank for yourself.

And while seemingly no family members or villagers were willing to consider the needs of this humble couple, there were shepherds out in the fields of Bethlehem working the night shift. If you ever get the opportunity to visit Bethlehem, you can visit these caves. They are just down off the hillside from the Basilica of the Nativity, which is built on the cave where Jesus was most likely born. The caves face Jerusalem and today, from their perch, you can see the scar of the walls between the Jewish settlements and the Palestinian people. The ancient and Byzantine chapels are left nearly untouched and unchanged for centuries. You can sit in the caves, with the ancient mosaic tile floors and images of angels and "Gloria in excelsis Deo" on the ceilings or walls. You can look over the hills and listen to the breeze. On any pilgrimage to Israel and especially to Bethlehem, make sure you stop and spend ample time at the caves of the shepherds; it will not disappoint. The last time I was there, I swear I either heard angels or their echo.

"Hark the herald angels sing. Glory to the newborn king. Peace on earth and mercy mild, God and sinners reconciled. Joyful all ye nations rise. Join the triumph of the skies. With angelic voice proclaim, Christ is born in Bethlehem. Hark the herald angels sing – Glory to the newborn king."

Once again, angels show up with a message for the humblest of people. We have moved from Zechariah in the Temple to Mary in Nazareth and now we are with shepherds in the hills of Bethlehem. These angels tell the shepherds of "good news" – in Greek *"evangelizo"*, the root of the terms: to evangelize and evangelism. Where Mary was to bear the Word made Flesh and bring the Logos into the world, these shepherds were the first witnesses to the good news of his birth and were told to discover the sign of his arrival.

Notice a few details from the angels' message.

They can find this baby in the "town of David". It's a small marker, but these shepherds know that the "town (Greek – *"polis"*) of David" is Bethlehem – while the City of David is Jerusalem. David had built his City of Peace – his "Jeru-salem" on the slopes beneath Mt Zion roughly one thousand years before the birth of Christ. Seeking to unify the twelve tribes into one nation, he sought to build a City where God could be honored and worshipped near where God has established His covenant with Abraham. After David's death, it was Solomon who built the first Temple up on the Mount of Zion and the City of Jerusalem has been connected to the City of David ever since.

And yet, when the angel tells the shepherds that the Messiah will be found in the "polis" of David, they know it's Bethlehem and not the capital. Interesting how a little bit of local knowledge goes a long way. By contrast, the brilliant astrologers who would come all the way across the Middle East by following a star would only get to Jerusalem, from there they would need the help of the local scribes to find the prophetic words of Micah that the Messiah would be born in Bethlehem. The star took them to Jerusalem, but God's Word brought them to the Holy Family. For all of their stargazing and time in the fields, these shepherds understood the message and knew where to look. They didn't head to Jerusalem and the Temple – they headed home, to the city of the shepherd King and to a stable.

But they were given another clue to look for: the baby would be wrapped and lying in a manger.

A manger was a food trough for animals, goats and donkeys and horses. A manger was kept in the stable, on the ground, full of hay and animal waste and hair. A manger is not a place for people to use; for any purpose. Let alone to place a newborn child. And yet, there it is. Right there off the lips of the angel.

The angel of God is both aware and comfortable with the second-person of the Trinity being in human form in a first century animal food bin.

Rejected by family and kin, left to fend for themselves, the parents of the incarnate God on earth are left with nothing but a wooden or stone box that usually contained the slop for animals to be the first bed for their son.

This is a most unusual sign.

But maybe not for shepherds. Maybe not for laborers working a night shift. Maybe not for people who aren't used to help from others or sanitized rooms or even dry beds. Maybe, in the same way that David knew he could kill Goliath because he knew that a slingshot was a better weapon from a distance than a sword; maybe these shepherds were a little more in tune with how God works. They knew what it was like to sleep in the crevices and find protection in the fern caves. Where they lacked degrees and formation and "catechesis" – they possessed something far more important to God:

Humble and open hearts.

And Luke tells us that they hurried off to find this sign – to see this child. And having seen him, they started to bang on doors and alert people to the angels and the message and music and the Messiah, just down the block, wrapped in a blanket and sleeping in a food trough.

If we are able, if we can put down our own sophistication and reliance on modern things for just a moment – if we can re-enter this sacred moment, there is such an invitation here.

What if God wants to soften and open up our hearts to lead with humility?

Can the things that have gone wrong for us in our lives shape us into people who are more open to God intervening in unexpected ways?

So much about this story is wrong from my view. I can't believe that Joseph put Mary up on a donkey and dragged her across the country just because of a tax code update. I can't believe that these relatives were so bitter and backwards that no one would assist this young couple in a desperate hour. Where is the compassion or hospitality or even some basic humanity? I struggle to believe no one else in Bethlehem saw these angels. Where were the priests or scribes or anyone with a degree or training or background to witness these incredible events? How did the King of Kings come into the world and the best that humanity could offer was a manger? Seriously?

But watch this –

Against all of this, the angels say this is "good news". They claim that this is going to bring great "joy" to all the people. All of this calamity is juxtaposed by angels singing about the glory of God and even peace resting on those who have found favor with God.

Mary and Joseph have found favor with God?

How? They are utterly alone, with no resources, apparently no friends or family, rejected – no plan. Nothing. Their kid was born in a cave and they didn't have anywhere to put him but in an animal's food dish.

AND YET – Mary teaches us:

"But Mary treasured up all these things and pondered them in her heart."

Against that wild backdrop, Mary does some internal work. She doesn't just display self-control and calm; she takes it all in and cherishes the picture. There are so many words in Luke's sentence that matter but I'm drawn to "all". All of it. The journey, the rejection, the animals, the manger, the shepherds' visit and their message; her husband and most importantly, her son – ALL of it.

Her labor. Her delivery. Her participation with bringing the savior of the world into reality. Her experience of the Divine in her womb and now in her arms. No one on earth knows what Mary knows in the way that Mary knows it – the physical experience of John's mystery: the Word made flesh and dwelling among us.

John's verb in his famous prologue was *skenoo* – literally "to tabernacle with". The word reminds of us God tabernacling with Israel for all those decades in the desert of Saudi Arabia. He had traveled with His people with His Presence in a box; a sacred Ark that both purified and terrified His people.

Now, God was once again "skenoo-ing" or tabernacling with His people – but this time, in human form. First as an embryo growing in Mary's womb and now in his sacred physical body as a baby born into a human family.

Only women know the physicality and reality of this glorious and mystical experience. Whether a woman has ever been pregnant or given birth, each month, she is keenly aware of the potential for life that starts in her womb and leaves her body. To be honest, men have literally no idea how to relate to what women experience: the invisible power of life from the womb.

And Mary treasured all of it. She had carried the Son of God in her body and she had been the Ark of Israel. God had tabernacled in side of her and the Word was made flesh through her labor.

And as she sat in wonder and awe of all that she had just experienced, she teaches us. Treasure and ponder the Presence of God in your life regardless of the circumstances and settings.

She had shepherds not family.

She had a cave and not a bedroom.

She had Joseph and not a midwife.

She was rejected by her husband's family instead of being embraced.

She was in a strange and unknown part of the country instead of in the comfort and familiarity of home.

But she treasured it all because she knew that God was present in her life and He had come into the world.

There is a juxtaposition here that I'm only able to mention from the fringes. Only a woman knows what it means to experience the reality of childbirth. I suppose there are some things that only a man experiences, but I don't know that there is anything that parallels or even rises to the level of childbirth. Taken a little bit further, what can be said for the gift of nursing – of literally feeding the life that has been nurtured and created in the womb. As a man, when I read that Mary was able to "ponder and treasure", quite honestly, I think I'm an outsider to that mystery and wonder. And so it's with great hesitation that I propose that Mary, a mother, uniquely experienced a cornucopia of thoughts and emotions at the birth of her son – let alone the physical trial of the journey and the labor.

When we consider all that this young woman bore – all that she carried in her body, mind, and soul – I stand back and marvel at her wordless capacity to treasure and ponder.

Luke has told us that he spoke to eyewitnesses. Given Mary's silence during the narrative, he either got her response directly or from someone that she told. You can imagine the questions – "What was that like for you, Mary? What were you thinking and feeling? Having gone through so much? With so much that went wrong and so much unknown?"

Mary's response: "I treasured it all and bound it all up and I tucked it away deep in my heart."

Wow.

This principle may seem a bit distant to us. Against such a gritty backdrop, Mary can seem almost other-worldly to us. Maybe a personal anecdote will help. Years ago, on a certain Wednesday in November, I was sitting in my parish office, about 20 minutes away from heading down to the 3rd graders. Each Wednesday I taught in the parish school and really enjoyed my time with the kids as I passed through their classrooms. They had energy and innocence, and the kids grew so much each year.

On this particular day, I took a call from a urologist and stepped outside. I learned that I had prostate cancer and that my wife and I would have to meet with him personally on Friday to learn about treatment options. I knew right away from the numbers that the only hope for me given my age, was a "radical" surgical removal of my prostate. Even then, my outlook was unknown. It was a total gut-punch and gut-check.

I was standing outside the church office. I checked my watch. Five minutes to third grade. Every Wednesday I read two chapters of CS Lewis's "Chronicles of Narnia" to them, and they loved it. And I loved their attentive reactions to the story.

What do you do when you learn that your whole life is on the edge?

I read Narnia to 3rd graders.

They helped me. They had no idea but their attentiveness and joy and curiosity calmed my heart and mind and I was able to start to move forward.

When I look back on learning about my cancer and reading Narnia to those kids, I ponder about that moment, and I treasure it in my heart. It was not a "good" day – except that without it, I would be a dead man. Walking with my wife that afternoon and telling her that I had cancer was not "good" – but the grace and beauty of her presence and her faithful response is something I treasure and ponder in my heart.

Thank God I had learned from Mary how to live into a moment and experience the Presence of God in the unexpected twists and turns that are part of life. Thank God I had sat with her for hours, considering her nativity and her capacity to absorb goodness in the midst of chaos. We will see her use this calm and strong determination again in the coming stories; most potently at the death of her son.

So how do we live this out? How do we apply this to our leadership?

In the old version of myself – in the Peter-the-fisherman version of myself – I would have identified what was wrong and taken active steps to rectify the obstacles. I would have made action plans to correct wrongs. I would have been an inner mess of thoughts and emotions, competing to find a faithful way forward to the mission while preserving what I thought both God and I deserved.

In this Marian world, we're invited into a deeper well of leadership. When circumstances appear strange or obstacles emerge, we are welcomed to acknowledge them and continue to sit and to move. When there is no room for us in the inn, we should open ourselves up to the stable. When those who *should* acknowledge and champion us fail, we wait and receive the praise and invitation from unexpected friends and voices. When no crib is presented, we flex and clean out a manger and find the simple beauty of a humble approach.

Mary leads us to find our joy and our contentment in the Presence of God and the joyous invitation to participate with Him in the salvation of the world. The invitation alone ought to humble us. Peter would learn humility through failure and trial. God bless him. How we love St Peter!

Mary seems to do things naturally and maternally. There is a tenderness and a strength and a power in her leadership that is second to none. Though I am more naturally wired to be Peter – stumbling through my failures and confusion, I sense this quiet and potent invitation to sit by Mary's side in Bethlehem and watch the Incarnation unfold.

Shepherds become prophets
Mangers become thrones
Small towns become the beacons of Kingdoms

Circumstances are proven to not be what they seem.

Reading Narnia to children becomes a balm to an overwhelmed and distraught mind.

In Marian leadership we find a depth that can only be discovered through grace. We've seen Mary's unique blessing in that regard. What can we do if we lead out of this grace?

Can we live out of our foundational essence as children of God AND invite others to join us? Can we help those we lead to find themselves fully in the grace of Christ as sons and daughters of the Lord God Most High – Beloved heirs of God and His Kingdom?

As children of God, can we fully surrender our lives to God and His Word in our lives? Can we put away our need to know "how" everything will be done and step into the adventure and mystery of WHAT He is doing and WHO it is that is asking us? Can we invite others to hear that same Voice and to respond "yes"?

Can we live our lives in counter-cultural confidence – building on the generations of people of faith who have seen reality for what it is? That the kingdoms of the world have failed, and that Christ is victorious through His life, death and resurrection and His Kingdom is an incoming and incarnate Kingdom that is both established and establishing? Can we live as St. Paul encouraged us – "to not conform any longer to the patterns of this world but be renewed by the transforming of our minds?" And can we model this way of thinking and living in such away that others are drawn and attracted to our counter-cultural confidence as children of God?

And now, with Mary at Bethlehem, can we approach daily life with humility, knowing beforehand that not everything will appear to go "our way" and that circumstances and obstacles will arise. Can we merge those unexpected and sometimes unwelcome moments with the reality of the Presence of God and experience the profound invitation to ponder who God is and what He is doing? And then treasure this juxtaposition because if God is going to tabernacle with humanity, then it is going to get messy. Can we begin to see life's seasons and challenges as windows into the Incarnation, the Word made flesh, the quiet and powerful witness of the Mother of God on earth?

And what if we invited others to do so? What if we helped others to see life and its reality in this way of the Incarnate God who chose shepherds and a manger?

If we begin to take our steps in this direction, then we are ready to hear Mary's last recorded words at party in Cana and the truly miraculous begins to open for us.

The Fifth Principle:
"Do whatever he tells you"
Living with obedience

For sake of brevity, we'll skip over the visit of the Magi, the Presentation in the Temple, the escape to Egypt, the return to Nazareth, the misadventures of the Holy Family's pilgrimage to Jerusalem and the utter silence of Jesus' young adulthood. Without a doubt, we could rest over each of those scenes and episodes and continue to glean pearls of wisdom. While not meaning any disrespect by glossing over these years, at a minimum we can observe that as Jesus' mother, Mary led a full and interesting life!

But as we re-enter the story, we find that with the help of his cousin, Jesus has gone public. By the banks of the Jordan River, he has taken on a few pupils, and we shift from Luke's steady hand to a new narrator– John the Beloved.

After spending "the whole day" with his new friends, John tells us that Jesus showed up with his small group of followers at a local wedding. Where Luke liked to drop ancient historical GPS, John prefers to drop signs and symbols. He tells us that this wedding took place on the "third" day in Cana and that Mary was already there.

Most scholars don't take the days literally, and until recently, traditionalists had the wrong village identified in the mountains behind Nazareth. Turns out the real Cana in this story is off in the hills to the north of Capernaum and the Sea of Galilee. John tells us that Jesus and his disciples had been invited to the celebration. The timing and location is important only because it shows the reach that Mary had in the geography. By car today, it would take over an hour to drive from Nazareth to this site. We don't know anything about the nature of the friendships here, but we know that Mary cared deeply for the family and that she had a ton of influence of the proceedings.

As the party continues, a cultural horror emerges. John simply states, "When the wine was gone..." This stain was unthinkable in the ancient world. Weddings and their receptions were celebrations that lasted for days, if not longer. Traditionally, when a daughter was born, the father would either plant a vineyard or pay to have one begun just to provide the wine for the party. To run out of wine was a sign of ruin and embarrassment. But there's more. John informs us that Mary tells Jesus: "They have no more wine."

In the ancient world, wine symbolized life. In the literal sense, the party is over– the family is dishonored– the father is disgraced. But in the spiritual world, Mary is telling Jesus that the world has no more *life*. We shouldn't read too deeply because we are dealing with

Mary the Mother of God and her son Jesus, the Savior of the world, but it appears, at a minimum that Mary is bringing this matter to Jesus for his intervention. Mary is letting Jesus know that this family is in trouble AND that the world has run out of life itself.

Jesus' immediate response is confusing and honestly, a bit dramatic. Taking in the scene, Jesus tries to stay in the shadows. Respectfully, He reminds Mary, this is not the time yet.

Obviously, they are having a conversation at another level. Given all that we've learned so far about Mary, we shouldn't be surprised. However, we do have to remember that this is also a conversation between a mother and a son. This moment is so incredible. "Full of grace" talking with "fully God and fully man".

We can discern that Jesus is looking further down the timeline, past the wedding reception, past the feeding of the 5,000, past the Sermon on the Mount– past all of it. We get a small window into Jesus' ultimate time– his *"chairos"* – there is a "time" that will come for Him and he wants Mary to know that this is not yet his time. I don't want to dwell here because there is so much question and uncertainty around Jesus' response. We can tether safely to the conviction that he is talking with Mary more about the fulfillment of his *life* – his blood – his *wine* being shed in atoning sacrifice on the cross than he is about the wedding host's fermented grape supply. But for our purposes, the next words are what are so surprising.

Given what Jesus just said – sort of a mystical "stand down" to his mother, John tells us that Mary, as perhaps only a mother can do, turns to the wait staff and utters her last recorded words in the Gospels:

"Do whatever he tells you."

As we digest these words, the action makes sense. Mary is concerned for her friends in the here and now. She wants Jesus to do something to help them. In the midst of that need, Jesus' reluctance is tied to the deeper revelation that the timing of his self-giving death won't be fulfilled until further into the future.

But Mary brings the story back to the here and now. She takes Jesus (and us) back to the present and in essence, uses her influence as a mother to initiate the saving actions.

We could imagine the story ending with Mary embracing him or encouraging him or praying with him. There are so many ways in which a mother can encourage a child in their vocation or their "path" or their journey. When our kids get starry-eyed about their horizons, our mothers can be incredible sources of compassion and steady encouragement.

But in this instance, Mary doesn't provide that emotional or stoic support. Instead, she activates him through the directive to the waitstaff. But here's the more surprising thing:

THE SERVANTS DO WHAT MARY SAID.

John's story continues with the most improbable of circumstances. Jesus, activated by Mary's prodding of the servants, concocts a solution to the diminished wine supply that no one could have imagined. He turns to the servants and instructs them to fill up six massive stone jars with water... to the brim. John wants us to know that it's a total of 120-180 gallons; that's more than a liquid TON of wine! And we're familiar with what these jars were used for – they had been used by the same servants to wash the feet and hands of the travelers who had come to celebrate.

Jesus's solution is so unreasonable and so dangerous and so humorous that it starts to take a narrative life of its own. How long would it take to fill 120-180 gallons of water with buckets or ceramic vessels? Who knows how far they were from the well or the spring, but this took time and effort. And beyond that, these "jars" were used for a cleansing purpose– they had been used to clean the feet of people who had traveled over hills and lanes that were dotted with animal manure and who knows whatever else.

Can you imagine the conversation among the servants as they made trip after trip with their buckets? I always wonder if Mary and Jesus stood to the side with smiles or if Mary gave Jesus a hard time that his solution involved so much labor. Either way, we know that the servants were uniquely in on the gag because John tells us that after the Master of Ceremony had tasted the water turned to wine, he was totally in the dark, but "the servants knew".

Imagine the look on their faces when the MC took a drink and came out praising the groom and his family. John gives us the impression that the servants were completely involved in the miracle. Jesus' actions not only saved the day, but also made his circle larger. John gives us the commentary to the moment, explaining that this was his first miraculous sign and through it, he began the work of revealing who he was to his disciples who began to believe in him.

The story ends with this nice detail:

"After this he went down to Capernaum with his mother and brothers and his disciples. There they stayed for a few days."

When the Voice of the Father called Jesus His Beloved at the Jordan River, John the Baptist had called out – "Look, the Lamb of God who takes away the sins of the world". A few of John's disciples began to follow him and they spent the day with him. Here in Cana, Jesus does the revelation himself and once again, the sign is followed by time with Jesus together.

John gives us a wonderful and tidy story. And the entire action hinges on Mary's words to the servants:

"Do whatever he tells you."

And here is where we come in.

We are the servants. We are the ones who are at the party, going about our work. We see the world and its issues. We can agree as witnesses with Mary– the world has "run out of wine". We all need to see God's glory revealed. We need Jesus to do things in our lives and in the lives of those around us. We need His life filled up to the brim– in us and in others.

But how do we do that?

How do we get to 180 gallons of the best wine ever served in town?

How do we move from shame and disgrace and emptiness to celebration and praise and fulfillment? And in our leadership, how can we possibly witness miracles in other people's lives if we barely have enough faith or grace for our own selves?

Let Mary teach you. Her instructions are clear and they are simple:

"Do whatever he tells you."

Obedience to Jesus can oftentimes be presented as obligatory. Obedience to the virtues of the Christian life or to the moral law of life in Spirit can often be conveyed in black and white terms. Deny the self and pick up your cross. Obey Jesus and not yourself.

But in Mary's encouragement, I hear something different.

"Do whatever he tells you because he is going to do something great and you will get to be a part of it"

Being invited by Jesus to do something is a privilege, less obligation and more invitation. Think of it, if it were gym class and Jesus was a team captain, wouldn't you be thrilled if he picked you from the line-up? Do you think you'd pause and say, "Nah— I've got my own ideas on how I want to do this thing."

This vision of inviting obedience is difficult to digest in the modern world. We are living in a time, an "era" where once again, the world is "running out of wine." So many institutions and leaders and cultural philosophies and messages are proving to leave people with no purpose, no meaning, with no real life. Our world is suffering through a endemic of meaninglessness. There are many identifiable dynamics that are causing this angst and interior suffering, but perhaps chief among them is the obsession with the self. Our contemporary worldview is deeply rooted in the Enlightenment and has moved far past the helpful and good dynamics that contributed to incredible advancements. Increasingly we live in a world that is unhinged from the foundations of self-less sacrificial love into a space that is chaotically orbiting around the self-centered discovery of the individual.

When we lead people with Mary's invitation to obedience, we are inviting them to freedom, freedom from the false philosophy of self-absorption and self-obsession.

With Mary's call to obedience, we are introduced less to a set of morals and more to a way of living and breathing. In a world where the pace of running out of life is accelerating, Mary stands up at the party and declares a way out:

"Do whatever my Son tells you."

So then what do we do?

Notice, Mary's invitation to obedience doesn't start with us. Our action follows her Son's word. Our action starts with our listening. He has to tell us something.

Mary's call to obedience starts with sincere and open prayer. This isn't an empty activism nor is it a call to justice without power. Mary isn't about correcting wrongs in an arbitrary manner – she is about revealing the glory of her Son that we might all believe more in Him as the Son of God.

What is the reward for our listening and our obedience?

We will put our faith more deeply in Him and we will increase our time away with Him and in fellowship with those who know Him deeply too. And notice, she'll be there on retreat with us as well.

What does this principle look like in our leadership?

I remember when I made this change. At one point, I was supervising about 6 full-time and 6 part-time ministry leaders. I would meet with the full-time people every other week and the part-time once-a-month. They knew that every meeting would begin with two questions:

1 – How is your soul? Describe it to me...
2 – What has Jesus been saying to you...

I can remember the discipline it took to ask those questions at every appointment. For sure, we had "business" to go over. There were leaders to be trained and kids and families to talk about. There were issues and monies to be raised. We all had a myriad of concerns and issues to resolve. But Mary taught me that we weren't in the "business" of problem-solving. We could solve problems and we could create strategies. These people were good leaders so they could even get people to follow them.

But what we wanted was something more. I wanted to invite them to see miracles. We wanted to see Jesus reveal Himself and to have our faith increase. I wanted us to be there when the most improbable and impossible happened – when water was turned into wine. I wanted us to be leading from the background, as waitstaff who were doing whatever Jesus asked us to do.

The hard work was to learn to listen. To slow down. To breathe. To be open. To become more familiar with His voice. To open our hands and our hearts.

But it gets easier as the impossible becomes real and His voice gets stronger as the faith increases. In fact, it's the times when He's quiet that can be the hardest. But its good to wait, His timing is perfect and just when you think the party is over, He tells you what to do.

So what about you? Are you ready to do whatever Mary's Son tells you to do?

The Sixth Principle:
"Woman, here is your son"
Living by being present in suffering

Perhaps there is no greater gap between Peter and Mary then in the events surrounding Jesus' death. That statement is no criticism of Peter; I am confident that I more closely identify with him. I'd be the one declaring my undying devotion only to ignorantly betray Jesus and myself along the way. I'm sure I would have spent Friday and Saturday weeping too.

But Mary – look at her – Jesus's mother. Right there. Right by his side. What a mother. I pause again and recognize her maternal nature because I've seen it in others, and I see it every day in my own wife. Again – no knock on the men or the fathers, but the mothers I know, the woman I live with, if their child is going to suffer, they are going to be there for them.

Let's not forget the setting. The kangaroo trial had been a sham. The Sanhedrin had met in secret during the night, on the Passover of all things! Early in the morning, the rulers had the guts to wake up Pilate and bring him out of his house to rule on Jesus. There had been conversations and deliberations and even the crowd was asked to put it to a vote. The mob cried out and Jesus was beaten, abused, mocked and sentenced for being who he actually was: the King of the Jews.

Crowds swelled as he and two other criminals carried their cross beams up the Via Dolorosa from Pilate's garrison to Golgotha – the town dump. They had passed under the Judgement Gate and were crucified on top of the quarry that had been mined to build the foundations of Herod's Temple. Jesus was literally killed on the "rock that the builders rejected".

When they nailed him to the wood of the cross, the torturers couldn't figure out how to share his linen clothes and so they played a dice game at his feet. John's Gospel gives us such a potent juxtaposition of the sacred Body of Christ in the midst of the grossest of human cruelty and insensitivity. John reminds us of the prophecy that Jesus was fulfilling, telling us that the soldiers were passive participants in something that was directed centuries earlier. Against this horrifying backdrop, John tells us:

Near the cross of Jesus stood his mother, his mother's sister, Mary the wife of Clopas, and Mary Magdalene. When Jesus saw his mother there, and the disciple whom he loved standing nearby, he said to her, "Woman, here is your son," and to the disciple, "Here is your mother." From that time on, this disciple took her into his home.

Think of the characters in the drama so far. Peter the denier. Judas the betrayer. Caiphas the power monger. Pilate the weak politician. Herod the mocker. The scavenger soldiers. The bloodthirsty mob. The scene is full of humanity's worst.

And then – there is a ray of hope.

"Near the cross of Jesus stood Jesus's mother…"

And she's not alone. John tells us that there are three other women there as well. Standing. Watching. Praying. Loving. Staring. Encouraging. Witnessing. Grieving.

We don't have the words of Mary or Jesus to show that she knew what would happen to her son, but we also don't have the words showing her protesting. She is just there. Present. Watching. Praying.

And Jesus gets to work.

One of things that people do as they get closer to death is to make sure everything is set for them to be gone so we shouldn't be surprised that we see Jesus doing the same thing here. As humanity's horror show begins to recede from the drama and Jesus's kenotic love begins to take center stage, Jesus gazes upon his mom and takes care of her.

John tells us that Jesus saw his mother standing there, by his side and he also saw John, "the beloved one" there as well.

As a widow, without her son, Mary was vulnerable. She needed family to give her value and worth in the ancient society. Having just lost the last of his earthly possessions, Jesus, the son of Mary, creates a new family. Mary will now call John "son" – and John will call Mary – "Mom". In the midst of such death and destruction, a new seed is being planted. A new chapter is being written. A new family is born.

While we could follow this trail of hope and love, what I want us to lean into here is Mary's presence to suffering.

I've found over the years that my desire as a leader is to shield people from pain and discomfort. Let's not fault the instinct to remove obstacles for others or to help people avoid pitfalls or unnecessary agony. But this is different. Life comes with reality. Tragedies occur. Many people's pasts are full of trauma and pain. There are incidents and moments in people memories that are etched deep, touching the very soul of those we lead and work with.

Death is a real part of life. Loss and grief take their toll. Unrealized expectations are a constant drain and an emotional tax on our best intentions. We could speak endlessly about unresolved conflict or conflict that went awry. Sometimes, the people we lead and try to love are simply suffering because life is chaotic and messy and tragic.

The cross of Jesus Christ presents us with scenes of beauty and love in the midst of horror and pain. Jesus' death on the cross ought to leave us in awe. The Passion is full of agony and destruction while leaving us with a sense of love, urgency and purpose. As the story continues in John's account, after a drink of wine vinegar, Jesus simply says, "it is finished", bows his head and surrenders his spirit to God His Father.

John tells us that out of a deeply embedded observance of the Sabbath, those who were present acted quickly to have Jesus' body removed from the cross and set into a tomb. To get the bodies down and to speed up the process of death, just in case the victims had simply passed out, soldiers broke the other two men's legs.

When they came to Jesus, they noticed he was already dead and instead, pierced his side with a lance which revealed a flow from Jesus' chest of water and blood.

This scene is rich with significant symbolism and points to the depth of the sacramental realities of what God did for us on the cross and how He intends to feed His "body" now that Jesus has died. But for our purposes, we want to see this through because for Mary – this was her beloved son and she uniquely knew and loved his sacred body. I watch the way my wife cares for my sons' bodies. They are nearly grown men now, but she has a nurturing and tender care for them that I simply don't possess. I'm not cruel-hearted but I simply know that I lack the beautiful and caring touch that oozes from her physicality and actions. I'm not suggesting here that all women are this way or that all cultures are so physically tender, but I am highlighting that Mary was painfully present not only for the Jesus' suffering and death, but remained so as Jesus' body was presented to her.

During the Renaissance, this moment and image became elevated. A young sculptor named Michelangelo was commissioned by a French Cardinal to sculpt the scene for his own burial. The statue became one of the great artistic gifts given to the world and is simply called "La Pieta" ("The Pity") and sits immediately to the right of the massive entry doors to St Peter's Basilica in Rome.

The sculpture is breathtaking in its beauty and a full demonstration of the young artist's inexhaustible skill. People travel from all over the world to visit St. Peter's. There are vast crowds every day. In order to get into the Church, there are queues and waiting and security lines. The size and scope of the Basilica takes away one's breath and the main altar and dome are almost other-worldly.

But upon entry to the grand Basilica, people are immediately drawn, like a magnet, to this modest sized sculpture that sits behind glass to the right. There is always a crowd gathered there, people kneeling or contemplating this agonizing scene of a mother holding the dead body of her son.

This is another terrifying picture of the reality of humanity, somehow made beautiful by Jesus and Mary.

People have written books on "La Pieta" alone, but for this moment, I just want to highlight that in Michelangelo's interpretation of the scene, Mary's left hand is off the body of Christ and open, palms up to Heaven – as if she was offering her son to God and to us.

Her face is young and flawless and beautiful. Her gaze is sad and focused. She is in pain. She is fully present with her son who is lifeless and she bears the weight of his death, physically and emotionally. While her right hand holds up his upper half – notice that her garments are wrapping his body and even she herself doesn't touch him directly – her left hand reaches out in surrender and offering.

John tells us that two members of the Sanhedrin, Joseph of Arimethea and Nicodemus worked with haste to wrap Jesus's body for the initial burial. To be certain, Mary and the other women were present and attentive to these efforts – we'll find Mary of Magdalene in just a couple of days returning early in the morning to complete the burial tasks.

But this in-between moment is uniquely Mary's. She surrendered her son to death and offered him to God and to us for our salvation.

Michelangelo's "La Pieta"

So much loss and so much beauty.

What does that mean for us?

How can we be present to those who are suffering? How can we begin to experience the redemption and salvation of God in the midst of the unfolding and horrifying reality of humanity?

When we think of our leadership and the lives of those we love and lead, let's make start with a few convictions.

What if we acknowledged the reality of pain and loss and grief? What if we became more aware of each person's story and history? What if we remained true to the conviction that while everyone is "new" in Christ, people's pasts are real and the Holy Spirit is always in the process of making people new and whole and healed.

Oftentimes, especially for those who are younger in spiritual leadership, putting on a Christian "mask" becomes second nature. While the tragedies and struggles of life are real and cumulative, we may sense a responsibility to the community of believers to remain strong and upbeat for the sake of others and to meet expectations. Leaders own needs can often be neglected out of a healthy and unhealthy desire to meet other people's needs in their own journeys. Sadly, there is a compounding effect to being available to a community of faith while neglecting our own realities and needs.

As people who grow and mature through this dynamic, the authenticity of Mary at the Cross and the image of "La Pieta" can speak to us.

There can not be long term health in leadership without the ability to integrate the reality of loss and grief into a healthy cycle of relationship and renewal.

As we take responsibility for leading and developing others, can we accept the invitation to enter into the world of their pain?

If we acknowledge this reality, then we need to learn and establish personal and professional boundaries. This might be the hardest step to learn and accept. As I grew in my understanding of Marian leadership– of being present with people in the midst of their suffering– I had to learn what my role was and what my role was most clearly – not.

In most instances, those entrusted to my care and leadership needed healing. They needed therapy. They needed spiritual deliverance. They needed assistance at the hands of a trained and trusted professional. More often than not, my role as being present to their suffering was to lead them to people and places of healing. I was not to be their healer myself.

In some moments, people's conversations with me or our shared experiences aided people in moving forward. There were times when burdens were lightened and people began to emerge from their agony. However, the real gift that my leadership began to provide was being present to their suffering and healing.

Mary's presence challenges us and teaches us. Can we stay at the foot of other people's crosses and watch them? Can we pray with them and for them? Can we wait and see what the Father will do? Can we hold them in the midst of their surrender and then offer them to God on their behalf?

And let's reverse the scene. Do we possess a small and tight circle of friends or family that watch us suffer? Are we trying to hide the crosses we uniquely bear from those who could encourage and pray for us?

A week after my surgery for cancer, my recovery took an unfortunate and painful turn. For a period of roughly 24 hours, I had bladder and abdominal pain that rivals the pain of childbirth. Without divulging the details, my bladder experienced contractions that would last 45 minutes to an hour for a 24 hour period. When we called the doctor's office, they said, "Sorry. Hang on and call us when it's over." As my body writhed and I struggled to retain control of my words, thoughts and emotions, my family was present for my suffering.

Because of the circumstances, it fell to my younger son, a boy of 14 years old to accompany me through the early hours of that agony. I could not hide it from him.

We had to ride it out together. He saw me at my worst. A scene that I would have begged to protect him from.

But my son, God bless him, was present with me.

He had learned from his mother how to be tender and prayerful and encouraging. I was not alone in my pain because my son was with me. Later that evening when my wife returned home and took over, it was her bedside presence that carried me through the night. A night of physical hell.

But here's the beauty of her presence. Years later, the pain is gone. My body is healed. While I have the memory of the agony, the more significant anchor that tethers my courage and my soul for these many years is the experience of the reality that my family was present with me in my pain. I was not alone.

Marian leadership calls us to move towards those who suffer. Following her footsteps means we place supreme value in being present with those we lead as they suffer.

What beauty could come if we grasped how important our presence is to those who are hurting?

Having held the lifeless body of her only son, what insights could she offer us as we encounter the mountain of raw human suffering and pain among those we lead?

The Seventh Principle:
"along with the women and Mary the mother of Jesus"
Living by corporate prayer

We are very familiar with the timeline and details of Jesus' death and resurrection. On Easter morning, He came out of the grave and encountered Mary Magdelene first, then took an afternoon stroll with Cleopas and an unnamed person (his wife who was at the cross perhaps?). Jesus' evening finished with the apostles locked in the Upper Room. He ended his big day with a fish dinner, probably steamed or grilled.

Luke tells us that He spent 40 days and nights with the apostles. St Paul tells the Corinthian church that Jesus appeared to over 500 different people during this period. But then, with very little warning, Jesus ascended into Heaven and the apostles were left, mouths wide open, gaping at the clouds.

Luke tells us that the apostles headed back to the City and the Upper Room. He takes a moment and does a roll call of the eleven. But then he tells us:

They all joined together constantly in prayer, along with the women and Mary the mother of Jesus, and with his brothers.

Typically, when we discover this little gem, we get excited or agitated about the declaration that Jesus had "brothers" which seems to disrupt the Catholic dogma regarding Mary's perpetual virginity. At the outset, I promised not to dive into dogmatic issues, but this one pops right out of the text and merits explanation.

The Greek word here is *adelphos* (ἀδελφός) and can mean sibling, but also is used to mean "brethren". This usage carries a broad meaning like "countryman" or even "associate". If I were to see a close friend of mine from college after a long time, I might embrace him and say, "Yo – brother (adelphos!) – how you doing?" This phrase or word is commonly used among people of faith, especially for those in communities of service like the diaconate or priesthood.

I'm not making a case here for Mary's perpetual virginity, I'm simply saying that this word and reference shouldn't be used as a point against it either.

But more importantly than that linguistic detail is the inclusion of Mary and the women in the dealings in the Upper Room. This cannot be overstated.

Imagine this moment for the Eleven; especially for Peter, James and John. Things were moving in such a potent and powerful direction. Jesus had restored Peter at the campfire in Capernaum. He spent the forty days proving his resurrection and teaching them about the Kingdom of God. What could have been better than that?

And then, unexpectedly, with little warning – WHOOSH! He was gone again. This time, very dramatically. Like the scene with Elijah and Elisha at the Jordan, except Peter isn't left holding Jesus' jacket.

There was talk from Jesus about the Spirit coming and power descending and their roles as witnesses, but it seems vague and unspecific. While they are chewing on these mysteries, they take the Lord's journey through the Mount of Olives; down through acres of centuries of old trees- trees that had witnessed all that Zion had to offer.

They took the winding road down the Mount. We have to wonder if they walked past the garden where Jesus had prayed on Holy Thursday. In that olive press of prayer, we have to consider that the memories may have been strong in their minds. And as they pondered these mysteries and what could possibly be to come, at that pivotal moment, the men decided that the women who loved Jesus should be invited into the "Upper Room".

There are many reasons why this moment is so earth-shattering and significant. Let's not forget that this is the first century. Women were rarely, if ever in the "room where it happened." On this day, the apostles made three choices:

Return to Jerusalem
Invite the women into the room
Replace Judas

The fact that Mary (Jesus' mother) is named speaks to her importance. The fact that the next ten days were engaged in fervent prayer is not insignificant either. Of course, none of us were there so we should not speculate on the conversations, but we can imagine the benefits of including the Mother of God who's last words were:

"Do whatever he tells you"

While we rightly consider the coming Day of Pentecost as the "birthday" of the Church, this brief 10-day period of waiting and corporate prayer was consequential for that movement of the Holy Spirit to even occur. If we consider the realities that the Apostles faced, staying holed-up in hiding in Jerusalem is an unexpected strategic move. We have to imagine the risks that the followers of Jesus were taking by staying in Jerusalem, especially with thousands of pilgrims and Temple-activity about to ascend on that ancient city. Everything in me would have wanted to sneak away back to safety, back to Capernaum or Nazareth or into the hills of the Decapolis. Even Samaria must have seemed friendlier!

Let's not forget that Jesus had just been brutally killed at the hands of the Romans and that the Sanhedrin had aggressively pursued his demise. Herod's Temple with its Roman garrison attached– literally to its walls– was THE power center of the Middle East. If they killed Jesus, it would have been natural to assume they would come for the Apostles too. Even more than that, Jesus had even told his followers to expect to "carry their own crosses". He had warned them that persecution was coming. At this point, I would believe him and everything in me would be working to keep myself and my friends off a Roman cross in the City dump.

Galilee would be so attractive. Galilee was the place were Jesus had done his miracles. It was the land of Encounter. Even after the Resurrection, Jesus had restored Peter on the shores of the Sea of Galilee. It was home; it was safety; it was heavenly.

If you've ever been to Galilee, you get this. Jerusalem is beautiful, but it is rocky and dry and hot. It is dusty and crowded; like the Psalmist says – it is a "compact city". But Galilee – Galilee is lush, it's fertile. It has a massive lake and refreshing breezes. Galilee has palm trees and lava rock walls. Galilee looks and sounds like Maui. Everything in me would have called me home, away from the Temple, away from the crowds and away from risk.

But God was doing something different. God needed those men and women to sit tight. 10 days. Just 10 days of waiting for something incredible. They could never have known what that would be. Jesus had told them that power would come upon them and that they would be His witnesses to the very end of the world – but in order to build their faith and obedience, he didn't tell them how. Pentecost is nearly as unexpected as Easter was!

Like Gabriel with Mary, we see Jesus laying the vision and being vague on the details. The only way forward is to stay in Jerusalem until the Power comes. And to make matters harder, he doesn't tell them that it will be 10 days. It's an unknown amount of time, with an unknown outcome with no specific instructions but with everything to lose. Yet he told them to stay.

Here's where Mary and the women's inclusion becomes so critical. Mary's last known words in the Bible is: "Do whatever he tells you to do."

We can sometimes mistake our Christian discipleship as a solo act. Perhaps this is the influence of our understanding of the "modern man" as an individual or perhaps it's the unique influence of Americanism, but the early church community is a different model.

This 10-day period is one of the most critical moments in the history of the Church... and in the history of the world! What an easy opportunity for the Apostles to take matters into their own hands. They could have easily justified a strategic move north and it would have not only made sense, it would have been valid. What could be smarter to keep their little movement safe then to move the base of operations to the north where they could control the landscape?

But God was bringing both the world and the Holy Spirit to them. He needed them to be his witnesses in Jerusalem in 10 days. He wanted them there and ready and listening. He needed them to hunker down and pray together.

For sure, there are moments where individuals hear the Holy Spirit and do heroic and unfathomable things. We'll see that in the Book of Acts when Peter responds to his dreams in Jaffa or when the Deacon Philip walks up to that carriage with the eunuch. Of course we see in the lives of the Saints, individuals encountering Christ and the Holy Spirit on their own and the most amazing things happen— fruit that lasts centuries.

While these examples do exist, taken as the whole, the Book of Acts is a story of a *community* of people who listened together to the Holy Spirit. That community extended through friendships and partnerships across the entire Middle East and the Mediterranean. Take a moment sometime and read the list at the end of Paul's letter to the Church in Rome. The early church was highly relational in its discipleship. They did what the Holy Spirit told them— *together*.

And so we return to the Upper Room in Jerusalem, 10 days before Pentecost. 10 days before the "birthday of the Church" except no one present even knows the plan, the script or the story.

In the midst of those gatherings, those times of eating, waiting and praying, who do we imagine was a leading voice? If they wondered if they should stay and wait, if they waivered in their commitment, if they began to strategize and feel the temptation to take matters into their own hands, who do you think was the leading voice to "do whatever he tells you to do"?

At a minimum, we can formulate that Mary, the mother of Jesus and her friends would have advocated for staying put and waiting. The fact that they prayed together is intimate and beautiful. We don't have those prayers. But we enjoy the fruit, the everlasting fruit of the fishermen from Galilee praying with the Mother of God awaiting the power of God to show up in their lives.

Mary was present and available to Gabriel and her "yes" made her pregnant with the Son of God. In the Upper Room, she was present and available again with the Apostles, and her "yes" made that group "pregnant" to become the Church it was about to become.

So what about us?

How do we face the unknown?

How do we equip ourselves when we live in our "10-days until Pentecost"? Each of us has a finite number of days on earth. Since we are people of faith, we know and believe that God is active in our midst and yet, we know that He is oftentimes light on details as the Spirit moves and He lines everything up. Christian history teaches us that sometimes His Spirit leads us to the "Promised Land" and sometimes His Spirit leads us to "Calvary".

Either way, have you journeyed that path of discipleship as a solo traveler? Or have you invited others to join you, at least in prayer?

There is tremendous power in praying together and to invite those who prayed in the Upper Room into our fellowship is even more powerful still. Inviting the women into the prayer circle in the first Century Judaism was beyond radical, it was unheard of. It begs the question of us today: who are we inviting into our circles of prayer? What would be the impact on our lives and ministry if we prayed with people who were different than us?

Consider what the author of Hebrews says:

"Since we are surrounded by so great a cloud of witnesses, let us also lay aside every weight and the sin that so easily entangles and let us run with perseverance

the race that is set before us, looking to Jesus the author and perfector of our faith."

Friends, the veil between our physical lives and the spiritual realities of the "cloud of witnesses" is very very thin. You are not meant to travel alone.

There is a temptation in leadership to face obstacles and difficulties with a great "plan" or strategy. Of course, these are crucial. But the power of the Upper Room Prayer Conference wasn't in the planning, it was in the praying. Consider our own leadership – are we calling people together to pray? Are we bringing in people that don't usually get invited to pray with us to listen and receive the gifts of the Holy Spirit?

What would happen if you invited Mary into your own Upper Room?

Post-Script
"Queen of Heaven"
The humble vessel becomes the Triumphant

Any Biblical survey of Marian leadership cannot ignore
the last time we see her. The Scriptures leave us this
nugget from Revelation 12:

*A great sign appeared in heaven: a woman clothed with
the sun, with the moon under her feet and a crown of
twelve stars on her head. She was pregnant and cried
out in pain as she was about to give birth. Then another
sign appeared in heaven: an enormous red dragon with
seven heads and ten horns and seven crowns on its
heads. Its tail swept a third of the stars out of the sky
and flung them to the earth. The dragon stood in front
of the woman who was about to give birth, so that it
might devour her child the moment he was born. She
gave birth to a son, a male child, who "will rule all the
nations with an iron scepter." And her child was
snatched up to God and to his throne. The woman fled
into the wilderness to a place prepared for her by God,
where she might be taken care of for 1,260 days.*

*Then war broke out in heaven. Michael and his angels
fought against the dragon, and the dragon and his
angels fought back. But he was not strong enough, and
they lost their place in heaven. The great dragon was
hurled down—that ancient serpent called the devil, or*

Satan, who leads the whole world astray. He was hurled to the earth, and his angels with him.

It is an understatement to say that John's Revelation is full of images, visions and symbols that point to both earthly and Heavenly realities that are beyond my capacity to understand. For this final encouragement, I'll just stick to what is plain.

As John takes us from scene after scene, Heaven to earth and back and forth, chapter 11 ends in Heaven. He tells us:

"Then God's Temple was opened and within his temple was seen the ark of his covenant. And there came flashes of lightning, rumblings, peals of thunder, an earthquake and a severe hailstorm."

Chapter 11 ends with a vision of the ancient Ark of the Covenant. We know that the Ark is lost to the sands of the Middle East. We know that the Ark was believed to carry the very Presence of God. Even when God's enemies got ahold of the Ark, they sent it back because it's power and potency wrecked them. Given Israel's own wayward history of disobedience, it's no mystery that they lost it themselves. Throughout much of Israel's tragic story in the Old Testament, Israel's leadership failed "to do whatever He tells you" and rejected Yahweh's kingship. In rejecting Yahweh and His

Torah, having a physical and potent reminder of God's very Presence would have been too much to consider.

The ancient Israeli Ark of the Covenant contained three physical items. These were the Manna from Heaven, the Rod of Aaron the High Priest and a stone tablet of the Torah given to Moses from God Himself.

These materials were physical encounters with the Bread of God, the High Priest of God and the Word of God.

In John's Revelation, he deftly moves from that Heavenly ark to our own earthly Ark – Mary the Triumphant and Glorious Mother of God.

This imagery helps us to understand that Mary is and has been the new "ark" of God. Within Mary's womb, she contains Jesus –

The Bread of God
The High Priest of God
The Word of God

In John's revelation, all the dust and grit and dirt of Nazareth and Bethlehem have worn off. John deftly pivots from the Ark of the Heavenly Temple to Mary – the Ark of the Earthly Incarnation – but notice the details of her image:

This is a "great" sign.

She is clothed... with the sun.
She has the moon... under her feet.
She has crown... with 12 stars.

I'll let the scholars get into all the imagery that follows, but we can be certain that this is the first volley in the Battle of Armageddon – the very final battle between good and evil, hell and Heaven, God and Satan.

At the end of Mary's introduction, John tells us that war breaks out: "in Heaven". By the end of the scene, we have the Archangel Michael hurling Satan and his fallen angels back onto earth.

We have come a long way from that humble and small home in Nazareth.

This Biblical image of revelation has shaped much of the art and imagery around Mary spanning centuries and cultures. For starters, we have to remember that these images are Biblical in nature. John was "in the Spirit" when he saw Mary as the "Queen of Heaven" at the dawn of the Battle for the End of all Things.

None of this deters from Jesus, the Son of God who appeared to John at the beginning of his revelation. Reread the first chapter of Revelation if you want reassurance that acknowledging Mary as the Queen of Heaven does not detract in any way to Jesus as the Lamb of God who takes away the sins of the world.

However, the first time I saw Mary as the Queen of Heaven, it did cause a reorientation for me around this figure from Nazareth. This vision is worthy of your own contemplation.

For me, I now look forward, with tremendous enthusiasm to meeting this person face-to-face in Heaven. I don't know how it works. Honestly, I haven't a clue. But I am hopeful that she'll let me approach her.

I'm not worthy to be in the presence of a person who is "clothed with the sun" and has the moon "at her feet". But she is a mother. She is full of grace. Perhaps given her willingness to spend time with the wait staff and fellowship with Galilean fisherman... maybe, just maybe she'd be willing to welcome someone like me into her court.

Let's be clear.

Mary the Mother of God stands at the forefront of the angelic armies of Heaven before the very final battle of good and evil. She is the opening salvo before her Son's final Victory, and her presence in this vision starts the battle.

And here is my final encouragement if we were to lead like Mary.

This Heavenly image is a current reality.

Mary already is enthroned as the Queen of Heaven. She is with you in your own most dramatic and tumultuous battles. She is with you and she is Triumphant.

Jesus is the King of Heaven.
But Mary His Mother, she is the Queen.

Why not take her into your battles with you?

She is full of grace. She leads from her essence. She is singularly surrendered to her Son and His will. She is a beacon of hope and counter-cultural purity against a dark and dismal world. She has been where you have been before and she is able to ponder all these things in her heart and teach you to do the same. She can lead you to a life of wonder, even in the midst of difficult and unfathomable circumstances. She will only tell you to do what her Son tells you to do. She can be present with you in your darkest and most horrifying struggles – never leaving you alone, but staying with you and rooting for you with beauty and dignity. She invites you to pray with her to her Son – who is present and hears everything prayed when "two of more come together".

She is your Queen of Heaven.

Wife of Joseph the laborer, she is poor, yet possesses everything. She fellowships with the most powerful women in history. Your salvation came through her very womb.

As I gaze on this final Heavenly scene, I like to imagine myself, just a small speck, staring from behind Mary and the Archangel and the rows of angels. Just a small human being, witnessing the incomprehensible. A small participant on the side of good versus evil. But present still.

Can you imagine the honor of being called into the realities of these unfathomable visions?

Crosses become lighter when we realize we are not alone and that Jesus and His Mother are triumphant and victorious.

The mantle of leadership becomes simpler when we join the cloud of witness and don't burden ourselves with the idol of individualism.

She is the Queen of Heaven.

What if she was yours too?

Also by Deacon Nathan Gunn:

THE WONDER WORKER

Buy on AMAZON TODAY!

A Rule of St. Nicholas
How to Save Yourself and Your Family from a Modern Western Christmas

Deacon Nathan Gunn
Forward by Msgr Bob Yeazel

About the cover art:

Bobbie Fetzer lives in Locust Grover Virginia.
Married to her husband Bill for over 52 years
she enjoys her sons and 8 grandchildren.
Bobbie has been writing icons for 15 years, primarily as a
means of personal devotion and worship. She wrote the icon
of St Nicholas for Dc Gunn's "A Rule of St Nicholas" as a gift.
Bobbie worships at Lake of the Woods Church
in Locust Grove

Made in the USA
Middletown, DE
23 September 2023

39032079R00066